WRITING
FOR
UNIVERSITY

POCKET STUDY SKILLS

Series Editor: **Kate Williams**, *Oxford Brookes University, UK*
Illustrations by Sallie Godwin

For the time-pushed student, the *Pocket Study Skills* pack a lot of advice into a little book. Each guide focuses on a single crucial aspect of study giving you step-by-step guidance, handy tips and clear advice on how to approach the important areas which will continually be at the core of your studies.

Published

14 Days to Exam Success (2nd edn)
Analyzing a Case Study
Blogs, Wikis, Podcasts and More
Brilliant Writing Tips for Students
Completing Your PhD
Doing Research (2nd edn)
Getting Critical (3rd edn)
How to Analyze Data
Managing Stress
Planning Your Dissertation (2nd edn)
Planning Your Essay (3rd edn)
Planning Your PhD
Posters and Presentations
Reading and Making Notes (2nd edn)

Referencing and Understanding Plagiarism (2nd edn)
Reflective Writing (2nd edn)
Report Writing (2nd edn)
Science Study Skills
Studying with Dyslexia (2nd edn)
Success in Groupwork (2nd edn)
Successful Applications
Time Management
Using Feedback to Boost Your Grades
Where's Your Argument?
Where's Your Evidence?
Writing for University (3rd edn)

POCKET STUDY SKILLS

Jeanne Godfrey

WRITING FOR UNIVERSITY

THIRD EDITION

BLOOMSBURY ACADEMIC

LONDON • NEW YORK • OXFORD • NEW DELHI • SYDNEY

BLOOMSBURY ACADEMIC
Bloomsbury Publishing Plc
50 Bedford Square, London, WC1B 3DP, UK
1385 Broadway, New York, NY 10018, USA
29 Earlsfort Terrace, Dublin 2, Ireland

BLOOMSBURY, BLOOMSBURY ACADEMIC and the Diana logo are trademarks of Bloomsbury Publishing Plc

First published in Great Britain 2011
This edition published 2022
Reprinted 2023 (three times)

Cover design: Friedhelm Steinen Broo

A catalogue record for this book is available from the British Library.

Library of Congress Cataloging-in-Publication Data

Names: Godfrey, Jeanne, author.
Title: Writing for university / Jeanne Godfrey.
Description: Third edition. | London ; New York : Bloomsbury Academic, 2022. | Series: Pocket study skills | Includes bibliographical references and index. | Summary: "This small, sharp and to-the-point guide shows students what academic writing looks like (and what it doesn't look like) and equips them with the tools and knowledge to tackle assignments with confidence"– Provided by publisher.
Identifiers: LCCN 2021047536 (print) | LCCN 2021047537 (ebook) | ISBN 9781350933675 (paperback) | ISBN 9781350933682 (epub) | ISBN 9781350933699 (pdf) | ISBN 9781350933705
Subjects: LCSH: Academic writing–Handbooks, manuals, etc.
Classification: LCC LB2369 .G58 2022 (print) | LCC LB2369 (ebook) | DDC 808/.0669–dc23
LC record available at https://lccn.loc.gov/2021047536
LC ebook record available at https://lccn.loc.gov/2021047537

ISBN: PB: 978-1-3509-3367-5
          ePDF: 978-1-3509-3369-9
          ePUB: 978-1-3509-3368-2

Series: Pocket Study Skills

Typeset by Integra Software Services Pvt. Ltd.
Printed and bound in Great Britain

To find out more about our authors and books visit www.bloomsbury.com and sign up for our newsletters.

Contents

Introduction

University study involves a significant amount of writing, whatever your subject. To produce a good written assignment and get maximum marks for your knowledge and ideas, you need to express and communicate them clearly and persuasively. Your written piece also needs to have a logical structure, an analytical and questioning approach, precise language, and source material incorporated in the correct way.

To produce a distinction-level piece of work you also need to demonstrate a level of creativity and originality that enables you to reach a (slightly) new way of seeing and addressing the assignment topic or question.

This pocket study uses examples of real academic writing and uses a 'show not tell' approach to take you quickly and clearly through all the essential elements of academic writing, focusing primarily on language. The guide shows you how to:

- write critically
- develop an argument
- use source material
- produce new insights
- emphasise your own 'voice'

- write clearly and precisely
- develop your academic vocabulary
- edit and check your work.

Writing for University shows you what your tutors expect from your writing and how to meet and even exceed these expectations. This book will help you feel more confident about your academic writing and help you make the best use of your talents and your time.

Myth	Reality
1 Being able to write well is a talent you either have or don't have.	Writing well is not a natural gift but something that you need to learn and practise. You may struggle at first because the style and content of writing for university is new to you but you will improve steadily and may even start to enjoy it.
2 There is one standard way of writing at university.	Many aspects of writing are common across subjects and assignment types, but you do also need to develop an awareness of the more specialised writing characteristics of your subject, task type and tutor's approach[1] (see Chapter 3).
3 You must find out everything about the topic and put it all into your assignment.	Your tutor wants to see that you can discriminate between relevant and non-relevant sources; in other words, that you can be selective in what you include in your assignment.

---

[1] Throughout this book I use *discipline/subject, task/assignment* and *tutor/lecturer* interchangeably.

4 Writing critically means saying what is negative or incorrect about something.	In the academic world, all knowledge and ideas can be questioned and there is rarely an absolute answer. Being critical means using this questioning process to evaluate information and ideas, and this evaluation might be negative or positive or both (see Chapter 5).
5 You should use lots of quotations.	The best way to re-express the ideas of other authors in your writing is by using your own words and style. You should use quotations sparingly (see Chapters 6–10).
6 Being original means coming up with a totally new idea or making a new discovery.	At undergraduate level you won't be expected to come up with a totally new idea but to reach your own view on an issue, which will develop from your unique thought processes and use of source material. At higher levels of study you *will* be expected to contribute to your field in some way, but this does not necessarily mean coming up with a totally new idea (see Chapter 11).
7 You shouldn't use 'I' or give your opinions.	Using 'I', particularly in your introduction and conclusion, is increasingly acceptable. Your tutor *does* want to know what you think, as long as you have formed your views through the analysis and evaluation of evidence and viewpoints from other authors (see Chapters 11–15).

8 You don't need to explain things that your tutor already knows.	At undergraduate level you usually do need to give relevant background information and definitions of key terms. You also need to explain clearly each point you make, even if you think your tutor should know what you mean (see Chapter 11).
9 Good academic writing uses long sentences and lots of long words.	Academic writing should be precise, clear and to the point. You should avoid using long sentences, and although you will sometimes need to use more formal words, you should not use unnecessarily complicated language (see Chapter 18).
10 Successful writers read, think, then write, then hand in.	Writing is a dynamic 'back and forth' process between thinking, reading and writing. Good writers often make lots of mistakes, and rewrite and correct their work many times before producing their final version (see Chapters 20 and 21).

PART 1
UNDERSTAND YOUR CONTEXT

2 What academic writing looks like

Below are the first two paragraphs and the first two reference list entries of an excellent second-year essay. At the sides of the extracts are comments that highlight good points about the essay's language and style (left-hand column) and about its argument structure and use of source material (right-hand column). Note that all of these features are important aspects of academic writing, regardless of whether you are writing an essay, a report, a case study, or any other type of university assignment.

Why do consumers buy organic and health foods? (2,500 words)

Language, cohesion, flow and style

Repetition of key words or similar words that help 'glue' the paragraph together.

There is a range of perceived reasons for consumer purchase of so-called 'organic food' (grown with limited use of fertilizers and pesticides and that arrives on the shelf without additives). Positive motivational factors for buying such produce are generally assumed to be the desire for better nutrition and health, and the belief that organic food is environmentally less damaging and therefore more sustainable than synthetic or production foodstuffs.

Argument development and use of sources

First sentence introduces the main topic of the essay and also of this paragraph.

Clear sentence structure that is formal but not too long or complicated.

Avoiding the perceived dangers of synthetic foods – pesticides, hormones and diseases such as salmonella and E-coli – is also an incentive to buy organic produce.

Links to the previous paragraph and also presents the topic of this one.

The evidence supports these assumptions of purchasing motives and, importantly, also indicates that there is no easily identified primary factor behind increasing sales. Two UK surveys (Avery 2006, Hallam 2003) found that the concerns of consumers who buy health foods include use of pesticides, antibiotics, food additives and fear of food-related diseases. Another study (Huber et al. 2011) found that perceived benefits to health were the most important motivational factor in buying organic produce. However, other research contradicts the findings of these three studies and suggests that health, food safety and care for the environment are not in fact strong motivational factors in consumers' intention to buy organic products (Michaelidou and Hassan 2008, Smith and Palasino 2010, cited in Çabuk et al. 2014). The issue, therefore, is whether we can identify any of the reasons for buying organic food outlined above as more important than the others and if not, what further …

Words that make links within and between sentences.

Formal words (but not overly so) that are precise and therefore powerful.

The student groups and summarises sources in their own words as support for their statement.

Student always references sources.

The student starts to explore in more depth the point they made in the previous paragraph.

References

Avery A (2006) *The truth about organic foods.* Chesterfield: Henderson.

Çabuk S, Ceyda T and Levent G (2014) Understanding organic food consumption: attitude as a mediator. *International Journal of Consumer Studies*, 38(4): 337–45.

Student gives full references at the end of assignment.

Understanding your context and purpose

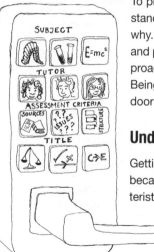

To produce a successful piece of writing you need to understand what your tutor wants you to do in the assignment and why. The three main factors in determining this writing context and purpose are the nature of your discipline, your tutor's approach to the subject, and your assignment title and/or task. Being aware of these will help you to unlock and open the door to more successful and effective written assignments.

Understand the nature of your discipline

Getting a feel for the character of your subject is important because different academic disciplines have different characteristics. Some disciplines, for example, put more emphasis on measurable data (quantitative evidence), while others will give more weight to interpretative, subjective evidence (qualitative evidence).

These disciplinary characteristics determine the types and purposes of assessment in the subject, so make sure that you understand what these are for your discipline(s). Below are some examples to get you thinking.

Discipline	Task type	Task purpose	Type of knowledge required
Art history, design	Written visual analysis	To analyse and evaluate a work of art in terms of the artist's technique and intended meaning. To discuss its cultural and social significance.	Personal and descriptive reactions supported by relevant theory, ideas and examples.
Biological science	Lab report	To propose a hypothesis and to report on the experiment conducted to test it, including the information necessary for someone to repeat it.	Detailed recording of methods and observations. Testable hypotheses. Completeness, thoroughness.

Discipline	Task type	Task purpose	Type of knowledge required
Chemical science	Literature review	To select and understand key sources, and to analyse, evaluate, compare and group them, thus identifying common themes and research gaps.	Evaluation of relevant studies to show current controversies, changes and gaps in knowledge.
Civil engineering	Case study report	To identify and/or propose solutions to problems in a real-life situation, using relevant theory and practice.	Detailed analysis of the case study scenario. Application of disciplinary knowledge to solve problems and recommend future actions.
Maths	Mathematical proof	To show the truth of a mathematical statement and demonstrate awareness of its implications.	Presentation of logical steps that demonstrate the truth of the statement.

Understand your assignment task

Your tutor wants to see that you have understood the point of your assignment title or task and that you have identified underlying assumptions and issues, so:

- ▸ try to read the assignment title and/or task brief objectively rather than just seeing what you want or expect to see.

- ▸ note that shorter assignment titles may look simpler but can in fact be more vague and therefore more difficult to interpret than longer ones.

- ▸ give yourself plenty of time (preferably a few days) to analyse and think about the assignment title/brief.

- ▸ discuss the assignment with your tutor and other students.

For more advice on assignment titles, see *Planning your Essay* and *Getting Critical* in this series.

Analyse your assignment task

1 **Break down your title or task brief into content, function and scope words (think of CFS or 'cuffs').**

   C: words related to the **content** of the topic. If anything is ambiguous, ask your tutor for clarification (but they will often want you to decide what something means).

   F: the **function**/instruction words. Read these carefully and check their meaning if you are unsure. If your title includes the words *argue* or *discuss*, ask your tutor for clarification, as there are different interpretations of these words.

   S: the **scope** – what you are asked to cover and not cover, for example specific time periods or countries. If the scope is not explicit (for example the title just says 'people'), you will need to decide for yourself what to cover and state this in your introduction.

2 **Think about the point of the assignment and what lies behind it:**
   - Why has your tutor asked you to write it?
   - What is the most contentious issue or aspect?
   - Are there any hidden questions or issues?
   - Are there any underlying assumptions or value judgements?
   - Are any cause-and-effect relationships implied and if so, can they be challenged?

Below is an example of analysing the assignment title for a discursive essay.

1 CFS breakdown

(F) Is it beneficial at all?

If it is beneficial, how much and in what ways? Try to keep the focus on how much and why it is beneficial.

(To what extent) is (global recession (good) for (law firms)?

(C) + (S) Define global recession. Do all global recessions have the same characteristics? <u>Don't</u> talk about local recessions.

(C) + (S) <u>Not</u> corporate lawyers or private solicitors.

(C) What does 'good' mean – financially? structurally? status? Can it sometimes be good for a law firm to lose business?

2 Notes on the point, issues and assumptions behind the title:

- Point seems to be to look at the relationship between law firms and global economics.
- Implied assumption is that law firms *are* affected by economics (supply and demand) just like any other business or industry.

And here is an example for a business case study.

1 CFS Breakdown

(S) Just one UK company (but it might source internationally).

(F) Stick to concise findings, not a long discussion.

(C) Definitions will be important including supply sequence. Need to state what aspects of infrastructure you will include (physical/social/economic/all?).

Select a UK clothing company. Report on its supply chain infrastructure, its approach to ethical sourcing, and the extent and methods by which it reports its ethical sourcing practices. Make recommendations for the company's developments.

(C) Include the 'what' and 'how'. Is there an overall strategy and how far down supply chain does it go? Different components? Involves other companies?

(C + S) You will need to define what this is. Stick to ethical, not other types of sourcing.

(C) Does it report everything? In detail? If not, what doesn't it report and why?

(C) Via official reports/ its own website/ advertising?

2 **Notes on the point, issues and assumptions behind the title:**

  ▸ Point is to use a real example to find out about supply chains and reporting methods regarding ethical sourcing, and to critically analyse the example and suggest improvements and future actions.

  ▸ Another point is to practise the format of a business report.

  ▸ An assumption is that all UK clothing companies do have some type of approach to ethical sourcing.

Understand your tutor's approach to the subject

Even within a single discipline, academics approach their field from different directions and might also have different ideas about what they want to see in a student assignment. Be proactive and ask your tutor what they consider to be the most valuable and interesting aspects of their subject. Your assignment marking criteria will often reflect these disciplinary and tutor preferences, so read them carefully and, again, perhaps ask your tutors which aspects of the criteria they consider most important.

For more advice on assessment criteria, see *Getting Critical* and *Planning your Essay* in this series.

Summary

- Approach your assignment as an opportunity to engage with the ideas and knowledge in your field and to produce your own response to the task.

- Check that you understand the point of your assignment type as well as the specific task.

- Tutors may differ in what they regard as the most important assessment criteria, so be proactive and find out what your tutor most wants to see.

- Don't make the mistake of reading your assignment title quickly, assuming you know what it means and then plunging into unfocused reading – analyse your title and instructions carefully.

Critical and non-critical writing

The term 'critical' as used in academic study doesn't mean making just negative comments about something but to think about it with a questioning attitude. The fundamental purpose of university is to help you develop this questioning, critical approach – to shake up your ideas and to 'make the familiar strange'.

More precisely, such critical thinking involves the whole process of analysing (breaking down) data and ideas, evaluating their strengths, weaknesses, relevance and value, and from this forming your own informed argument and perspective.

Pay particular attention to the 'analysis' part of your critical approach – breaking down and examining the different aspects and components involved in the terms, concepts and evidence. If, for example, you are writing an essay about business ethics, you will need to ask yourself questions such as:

- *What is a business?*
- *Are there different types of businesses?*
- *Is there a difference between a business and a charity?*
- *What are ethics?*
- *Are there different types and categories of ethics?*
- *Can you have a business with and without ethics?*

Your analysis of concepts will help you generate your assignment content and structure (see Chapter 16) and looking at ideas from new angles will also help you arrive at original insights.

A common reason for low marks in student assignments is having too much non-critical content (background information, description and explanation) and not enough criticality, particularly rigorous analysis followed by evaluation. You usually will have to provide a certain amount of background description, but it should be kept to a minimum.

Below are some extracts from a student essay showing the difference between non-critical and critical writing. The extracts are taken from an essay on the topic of ageism (prejudice or discrimination on the grounds of age).

Non-critical writing

Description

Descriptive writing gives the 'what' of something but does not analyse, explain or evaluate, and it does not try to persuade the reader of anything.

Example:

> The causes of ageism were first suggested by Butler (1969); a lack of understanding of older people, combined with fears about becoming old and a consequent desire for distance from old people.

Explanation

Explanatory writing can be mistaken for a type of critical writing because it gives the 'why' and 'how' of something and perhaps a conclusion; however, explanation is still non-critical because it is stating fact. An explanation does not analyse, evaluate, argue or try to persuade.

Example:

> Ageism often occurs because people develop unconscious negative associations with old age, thereby strengthening conscious negative attitudes and behaviours towards old people.

Critical writing

Analysis

Analysing involves taking apart a statement, concept or argument in order to examine and define it in detail.

Example:

> In their model of causes of ageism, Perdue and Gurtman (1990) emphasise the role of negative mental associations. However, associations are not the same thing as actual negative behaviour towards old people.

Evaluation

This involves weighing up the evidence and/or argument, and deciding on its validity, value, relevance and implications.

Example:

> A weakness in Perdue and Gurtman's argument is the claim that negative associations are unconsciously learnt at an early age, because this has not in fact been proven. Nevertheless, the phenomenon of negative association is important because …

Argument

An academic argument will include analysis and evaluation within it, as it is the whole sequence of an initial claim (also called a 'proposition') followed by supporting evidence, logical reasoning and conclusions. The function of an argument is to try and persuade the reader to agree with the initial proposition, and usually takes the whole piece of writing to develop. Below are just the concluding sentences of the student's whole argument.

Example:

> Although the extent of unconscious negative associations with older people can be debated, the evidence discussed here shows that they do exist. These associations are harder to address and redress than conscious prejudice and this makes them a disproportionally damaging aspect of ageism in our society.

5 Things to avoid

Below are examples of the types of statements you should avoid making when writing critically and developing arguments. Each example is annotated with an explanation of what the problem is and a suggestion of how to fix it.

1 Terms that are not precise enough

This essay has demonstrated that growth in international trade requires improved legislation to control monopolies.

Problem The statement lumps together all the different types of international trade and monopolies. (See also point 9 below.)

Solution The terms need to be broken down and then used more precisely. For example, the report could discuss intra-industry, inter-industry, intra-firm and inter-firm trade. If the student means all of these, they should make this clear.

2 Overgeneralisation

Countries need to improve the connectivity of their transport systems.

 WRITING FOR UNIVERSITY

Problem This statement is 'all or nothing' and is vague and therefore unlikely to be correct.

Solution Be accurate and specific. Statements should be evidenced and/or modified to reflect the complexity of reality by using phrases such as *most* or *some*. (See also Chapter 15.)

3 Unsupported views

This essay has presented valid arguments both for and against stem cell research, and it seems that such work is vital.

Problem This sentence gives an unsupported view. The fact that the student has presented arguments on both sides does not logically support her final opinion.

Solution Analyse and evaluate evidence to reach an informed position. In the assignment, present and discuss the evidence in a way that supports this view.

Tutors *do* want to know what you think, but only as an informed view, position or perspective.

4 Opinions that are then presented as fact

Animal testing is thought by some to be necessary. This paper shows that even though such testing is needed currently, the pharmaceutical industry is making good progress in developing effective, alternative testing methods.

Problem The first sentence presents the opinion that some people think animal testing is needed, but the second sentence turns this opinion into unsupported fact.

Solution The second sentence should say something like *'testing is perhaps needed'*. Alternatively, evidence for need could first be presented, making it valid to then claim this need as fact.

5 Conclusion given before the evidence

Using big data has substantial benefits for companies. This report analyses the advantages and disadvantages of using big data for large companies.

Problem The answer (that big data has benefits) is assumed before the supporting evidence has been given.

Solution Present your evidence first and from this draw your conclusion. You can start with a thesis statement, but it should include phrases such as 'I will argue/suggest/attempt to show that ...'

6 Steps in reasoning that do not follow logically (non sequiturs)

Identity theft is increasing; therefore, the government should introduce identity cards.

Problem There is no explanation of how the introduction of identity cards would reduce identity theft.

Solution Show clearly why/how your steps in reasoning follow on from each other.

7 Empty, circular argument

The government should instigate an 'opt-out' system of organ donation. This will ensure that a person's organs are automatically available for donation unless they have specified otherwise. Therefore, this legislation should be introduced as soon as possible.

Problem There is no reasoning in this argument, as the second sentence just defines an opt-out system, and the last sentence merely paraphrases the first.

Solution The argument should not begin with unsupported opinion but should develop via evidence and explain *why* automatic donation is beneficial.

8 Assumption of a causal correlation or connection

Children who play violent computer games commit more violent acts; therefore, the violence portrayed in computer games causes violent behaviour in children.

Problem The cause and effect link has been assumed rather than proven – the existence of a correlation does not necessarily imply causality.

Solution Either provide evidence for causality or describe the connection as a possibility only. Other possible explanations should also be described and evidenced.

9 'Empty persuaders' and subjective language

Euthanasia is clearly terrible because it involves killing people.

Problem The word *clearly* is used here to suggest the existence of evidence without actually giving any. *Terrible* is a subjective term and is meaningless without definition in this context.

Solution Words/phrases such as *there can be little doubt* and *obviously* do not prove anything. *Clearly* should only be used with evidence. Subjective terms such as *immoral* and *horrible* are not appropriate in academic work. (See also Chapter 18.)

Summary

- 'Taking a critical approach' refers to the whole process of analysing, questioning and evaluating evidence and your own ideas in order to reach a reasoned and informed position.

- Make sure you spend time conducting a rigorous analysis of concepts and evidence *before* evaluating them.

- You may feel that it isn't right or possible to question what experts in your field say, but taking a critical approach to ideas and research in your subject is one reason you are at university.

- In academic study you are expected to question everything, and this can be hard work – if your brain hurts a bit, you're doing it right.

There are two ways of using source information in your writing:

1 using the *exact words* of the source = quotation
2 putting the source information/ideas into *your own words* = paraphrase

Whenever you are about to use a source, ask yourself:

▶ Why do I want to use this source and how does it relate to the assignment brief?

▶ Do I understand it properly?

▶ Have I analysed and evaluated it?

▶ How am I going to use it to develop my argument and what do I want to say about it?

The difference between 'citation' and 'reference'

A 'reference' refers to giving details of a source such as the author's name and year of publication. A 'citation' is a wider term and can refer to both publication details and/or the use of source material as quotation or paraphrase.

Quotations are exact phrases or sentences taken from source material. Here is an example of a short quotation a student has used in a sentence in their essay about business ethics:

> A second, even stronger argument for the view that businesses should be ethical is that 'good ethics is synonymous with good management' (Collins 1994 p. 2).

Only use quotations for special occasions

Only quote if you feel that you have found a powerful or unique phrase, or if you need to give the reader the original wording before you go on to discuss it. The number of quotations you use will vary according to your discipline and assignment type – you might use quite a few in a literature essay but none for a laboratory report. As a general rule, only use short quotations once or twice a page at most.

Good uses for quotations:

- ✔ to state a fact or idea that the author has expressed in a unique and powerful way
- ✔ to establish or summarise an author's argument or position

☑ to provide an interesting or important start or end to your assignment

☑ to give the reader an original extract that you then discuss.

Don't use quotations just because:

☑ you think that putting them in will impress your tutor

☑ you haven't given enough time to reading and making notes and so have pasted source text into your assignment rather than trying to re-express the material in your own words.

Using a quotation: important points

1 Introduce it correctly

To introduce a quotation, either use the author's family name as the subject of your sentence and therefore without brackets, or keep the author's name out of your sentence and put it in brackets after the quotation.

Example:

Benjamin (1970 p. 41) argues that 'no translation would be possible if in its ultimate essence it strove for likeness of the original'.

or

> The translator should not attempt to copy the original exactly because 'no translation would be possible if in its ultimate essence it strove for likeness of the original' (Benjamin 1970 p. 41).

2 Use the correct punctuation

Use a colon if you use an independent clause (one that could stand as a complete sentence) to introduce a quotation.

Example:

> Winterson (2005 p. 3) uses the sea as a metaphor for life: 'Shoals of babies vied for life'.

Use a comma if you use a dependent clause (one that can't stand alone) to introduce a quotation.

Examples:

> As Tomalin (2010 p. 148) states, 'Pepys was … mapping a recognizably modern world'.
> According to Brandon (2008 p. 151), 'History is a record of relationships'.

Don't use any punctuation if you integrate a quotation smoothly into the rest of your sentence.

Examples:

> Polkinghorne (2002 p. 10) describes a quantum as 'a kind of little bullet'.
> One of Oswald's most important findings is that 'joblessness is a major source of distress' (Oswald 1997 p. 1825).

3 Indicate any changes you make

▸ The only alteration you are allowed to make without indication is to change the first letter in the quotation from upper to lower case so that it integrates smoothly with the rest of your sentence. Don't change lower case letters to upper case.

▸ Don't change the wording of a quotation. If the original has a spelling or grammatical mistake, keep it and insert [sic] after the word that contains the error to indicate that the mistake is in the original text.

▸ If you leave something out of the middle or end of a quotation, insert three spaced dots (called 'ellipsis') to show that you have done so. You don't usually need to use ellipsis at the start of the quotation if you integrate it into your own sentence. There are some usage variations, however, so check your course style manual.

▸ If you need to add anything to the original so that the meaning of the quotation is clear to your reader, use square brackets [ ] around whatever you add.

▸ If the original section you quote already has a quotation within it, show this by using single quotation marks for the main quotation and double quotation marks for the inside one (note that American English uses the reverse order).

Let's look at an example of using a quotation that demonstrates all of the above:

Source extract:

> This use of percentage GDA signals on front-of-pack labelling has been promoted by some sections of the food industry as an alternative to a 'traffic-light' signposting system recommended by the Food Standards Agency (FSA).
>
> Lobstein T, Landon J and Lincoln P (2007) *Misconceptions and misinformation: The problems with Guideline Daily Amounts* (GDAs). National Heart Forum report.

Student quotation:

> Lobstein et al. (2007 p. 1) state that 'use of percentage GDA [Guideline Daily Amounts] signals … has been promoted … as an alternative to a "traffic light" signposting system'.

4 Show that it *is* a quotation

For short quotations (up to two lines) you must use quotation marks. You can use either single ' ' or double " " quotation marks but use one type consistently.

For longer quotations don't use quotation marks. Instead, use a colon and indentation.

Example:

In law, as Wagner et al. (2011) state, where there is no *active* termination of life, it may not be unlawful killing:

> the law draws a crucial distinction between cases in which a doctor decides not to provide, or to continue to provide, for his patient treatment or care which could or

might prolong his life, and those in which he decides, for example by administering a lethal drug, actively to bring his patient's life to an end.

5 Check that your quotation is relevant and integrated

Comment on your quotation and show clearly why it is significant to your argument.

Extract from student essay:

A second, even stronger argument for the view that good ethics in business do exist, is that given by prominent experts on the subject: 'good ethics is synonymous with good management' (Collins 1994 p. 2). Collins' view is borne out by examples of businesses that are successful in part because they focus on the human element of management, such as …

This sentence introduces the quotation and shows how the student is using it to support their own point.

The student is about to give concrete examples as further support for their own point that businesses can be ethical.

Common mistakes when using quotations

❌ A key finding in the study was that 'the first variable, communication skills, was only indicated in 27% of the jobs listed' (Koong et al. 2020 p. 25).

> **What's the problem?** This quotation is not expressing anything particularly special or powerful, so the student should have re-expressed it in their own words, i.e. as a paraphrase (see page 43 for an example).

❌ The main benefit of organ transplant is that it saves lives. As stated by Smith (2005 p. 12), 'heart transplantation can save lives, but the procedure carries serious risks and complications and a high mortality rate'.

> **What's the problem?** This isn't a relevant quotation because the second part of it contradicts the point the student is making.

❌ Hairshine.com conducted a survey on the product. The survey showed that '82.7% of the interviewees were satisfied with the product and 10% were not satisfied' (Marchant 2021 p. 20). Customer satisfaction should be a priority for all companies …

> **What's the problem?** The statistics are not special enough to quote. Another problem is that the student does not evaluate and/or comment on them.

X Using animal organs for transplantation is beneficial, as patients are not forced to wait as long for transplants. As stated by Kline (2005 p. 53), 'advances in genetic techniques mean that there is less chance of animal organs being rejected by the human immune system'.

What's the problem? The quotation does not relate to the student's point about reduced waiting lists.

Using your words: paraphrase and summary

Paraphrasing sources

Paraphrasing is when you re-express someone else's speech or writing in your own words at about the same level of detail. Paraphrasing allows you to:

▶ restate the information or idea in a way that supports your own argument

▶ show your tutor that you have understood the source material

▶ restate the information or idea more clearly and simply

▶ express the information or idea in your own style so that it fits smoothly into your own writing.

You will usually only want or need to paraphrase one specific idea and/or a short section of text.

Example

Original text:

> The first variable, communication skills, was only indicated in 27% of the jobs listed.

Koong KS, Liu LC and Liu X (2020) A study of the demand for information technology professionals in selected internet job portals. *Journal of Information Systems Education*, 13(1): 25.

Student paraphrase:

The most surprising finding in the 2020 Koong et al. study was that from all the job adverts analysed, less than 30% gave good communication as a required skill (p. 25).

Summarising sources

You will often want to summarise the main points or ideas contained in a longer section of text or in a whole text. An effective summary is one in which you re-express the key points in your own words and style, although you might occasionally incorporate short quotations.

Summarising allows you to:

▶ restate the main ideas in a way that supports your own argument
▶ show your tutor that you have understood the key points of the source text
▶ restate the key information and ideas more clearly and simply
▶ express the key points in a style that fits smoothly into your own writing.

As an example, below is a section of a third-year undergraduate essay in which the student re-expresses the key point of a whole journal article by Professor Andrew Oswald titled 'The economics of happiness':

Oswald (1997) argues that economic performance does have an effect on personal happiness, but that the degree of happiness depends more on whether or not you have a job than on how much or little you earn.

You will often want to give a very brief source summary to contrast or group several different sources, re-expressing their key points in just a sentence or phrase. As an example, below is the introduction of a student laboratory report in which the student summarises three sources:

Anthocyanins are responsible for a variety of colours in flowers, leaves, fruits and vegetables, especially blue, red or purple (Patras et al. 2010). Because of their structural instability, anthocyanins can be affected by pH, temperature, light and bleaching compounds (Farr et al. 2018). Sulphur dioxide, which is often added to foods to inhibit enzyme-related oxidation processes, can bleach food, causing its colour to fade (Lindsay 2017).

Tips for effective paraphrasing and summarising

1 Read, reread and make notes on your source material until you understand it really well.

2 As you make notes, start to use your own words and phrases. Have a system in your notes for recording which bits are your own words and which phrases are from your source material. You need to record these differences so that you don't accidentally plagiarise when you use your notes to write your assignment.

3 Write your paraphrase or summary from your own understanding of the material and from your notes rather than continuously looking back at the original text. For summaries, initially try to encapsulate the point of the text in just one or two sentences – you can go back and write a more detailed summary later if you need to.

For more advice on making notes, see *Reading and Making Notes*, *Getting Critical* and *Referencing and Understanding Plagiarism* in this series.

4 Useful techniques to help you re-express material in your own way are to change or even reverse the original order of information and to use different word forms (e.g. decision-making → making decisions).

5 When you have integrated your paraphrase or summary into your writing, check that you haven't accidentally changed the meaning of the original text.

6 Check that you have stated clearly how your paraphrase or source summary supports your own point. Comment on your paraphrase or source summary either before and/or after it, not in the middle, as this will confuse your reader.

7 Having lots of small paraphrases is not good academic practice, even if you reference them all. If you find you are doing this, you probably need to summarise and group your sources more, and focus on discussing how they support your own argument.

> **Attention!** Using your own words and style does not make the ideas or information contained in the source yours, so always reference a paraphrase or source summary. (See Chapters 12 and 13.)

How much should you change the original text?

This is really the wrong question. If you follow the steps on pages 43–45, you shouldn't need to ask yourself whether you have made enough changes from the original text (although you may occasionally need to check this before handing in).

A paraphrase should be at about 90% your own words, sentence structure and style – a 'half and half' approach, where you 'stitch together' source words or phrases with a few of your own words, is **not** acceptable.

It is also **not** acceptable to change all the words one by one; an author's sentence pattern and vocabulary combine to create their own writing style, and so you must use *your* own sentence pattern and writing style.

Below are three student paraphrases of the same source extract. The first two paraphrases have not been properly rewritten and would count as instances of plagiarism – only the third paraphrase is acceptable.

Source extract:

> RRI [EU report *Responsible Research and Innovation*] referring to a broad policy vision to better align science and society, not only emphasizes public engagement as an

integral part of innovation trajectories but also demands that institutions of science and technology become more responsive to societal needs, issues and concerns and include these issues in decision-making processes.

Krabbenborg and Mulder (2015) Upstream public engagement in nanotechnology. *Science Communication*, 37(4): 452–84.

Student paraphrase 1: ✗

The order of information, sentence pattern and about half the text is unchanged (underlined).

> Krabbenborg and Mulder (2015) state that the EU RRI report <u>referring to a broad policy vision</u> to better <u>align science and society, emphasizes</u> not just <u>public engagement as part of innovation</u> but also asks that <u>institutions</u> that deal with <u>technology and science</u> respond more to <u>societal needs, issues and concerns</u> and include these when making decisions.

Student paraphrase 2: ✗

> Krabbenborg and Mulder (2015) discuss an EU report that <u>refers</u> to a wide <u>vision</u> of linking <u>science and society</u>. The report <u>emphasizes</u> not just <u>public engagement as part of innovation</u> but also asks that organisations that deal with <u>technology and science</u> respond more to society's <u>needs, issues and concerns</u> and include these when making decisions.

Still too many phrases from the original and this paraphrase still has exactly the same information and sentence pattern as the original text.

Student paraphrase 3: ✓

In this first sentence the student states their own point before giving the paraphrase as support.

The student uses the source to provide support for their point. The paraphrase integrates smoothly into the student's writing, and the words, order of information and sentence patterns are the student's own.

Technology and scientific institutions have no excuse not to realise the importance of including social and political contexts when making policy and strategy decisions. Krabbenborg and Mulder (2015) discuss the literature that is available to guide organisations, such as the 2015 EU report *Responsible Research and Innovation*. The authors point out that such reports also highlight the importance of public involvement in science in guiding the direction of new developments.

8 Using verbs to show you understand your sources

When you use or discuss other people's work, you need to use appropriate verbs and phrases that convey correctly what the source says and does. These verbs are often referred to as 'reporting verbs'.

Common reporting verbs

argue	demonstrate	provide
address	describe	point out
assert	discuss	portray
challenge	examine	question
conduct	explain	show
conclude	highlight	state
convey	identify	suggest
claim	investigate	trace
define	list	reject
deny	propose	

Use the right verb for the job

Using the correct reporting verb allows you to represent the source precisely and shows your reader that you understand what an author is doing. Using the wrong reporting verb will mean that you have misrepresented the source. For example, the two sentences below say different things about Georgiou 2021:

Georgiou (2021) describes the different uses of pain-relieving drugs.
Georgiou (2021) questions the different uses of pain-relieving drugs.

To help you choose the right verb, ask yourself what the author is trying to do – are they trying to inform their readers, to explain, recommend, persuade or something else? Moreover, within their overall aim, the author will be trying to do different things in different parts of their text. They may, for example, describe and explain, then analyse, challenge and finally discuss and conclude. So, make sure you understand what your source authors are doing in each part of their text.

Use the right grammar for the verb

In the active form, reporting verbs usually use one of three structures.

Commonly used structure	Example
verb + noun	Research data *challenges the assumption* that there is …
verb + that	Cote and Morgan (2002) *proposed that* job satisfaction is linked to regulating emotion.
verb + what/why/where/who/ whether	Lin and Moon (2019) *show why* the public is interested in medical stories.

Most verbs commonly use a particular structure, but some (e.g. *show*) can use all three. Try to notice how reporting verbs are used in the texts you read, and check the correct grammatical structures if you are unsure.

Check your use of reporting verbs

Kerlinger (1969 p. 1127) quotes that '"Science" is a misused and misunderstood word'. ✗ Shaw quotes Berringer to illustrate the point that 'companies will not survive if they do not adapt' (Berringer 2019, cited in Shaw 2021 p. 76).✓	Use *quote* only to describe when one author quotes another.
As Huai-Ke Guo et al. cite, gravitational waves have become 'a new cosmic frontier' in particle physics (2021 p. 2). ✗ Huai-Ke Guo et al. (2021) cite Scherrer and Turner (1985) to support their claim regarding the radiation cooling rate. ✓	Use *cite*[2] only when one author cites another author.
To summarise Karlov's main argument, he mentions ✗ / states ✓ that playing chess uses a similar part of the brain as playing music.	Only use *mention* to report minor points, not important ones.

---

[2] To 'cite' means to mention an author in some way – as a quotation or just by name.

Manzano et al. (2020) discuss about ✗/ discuss ✓ the increase of antimicrobial resistance and …	*Discuss*, *describe*, *define*, *study*, *examine* used as reporting verbs are not followed by a preposition.
As implied ✗ / stated ✓ by Murtaz (2007 p. 1), 'patient care should be the primary motive for developments in the NHS'.	Murtaz's statement is explicit, (something he has said openly) not just implied. The student should therefore have used a verb such as *state*, *argue* or *assert*.
The ideas portrayed ✗ / conveyed ✓ in the report are not new.	The student meant *conveyed*, meaning 'communicated'. *Portrayed* means to represent or describe in a particular way.

All referencing styles fall into one of two categories, author/year or numeric. Below is a basic summary of these two groups, with an in-text example in the left-hand column and a reference list example in the right-hand column.

1 Author/year system

The three main author/year referencing styles are Harvard, APA and MLA. For all of these styles, you should give the author's **family name** and year of source publication in the body of your assignment. In your list of references, you should list all the sources you have used in alphabetical order of the author's family name.

Example using Harvard referencing style

In the body of your writing	In your list of references
Lupton (2021) states that there is a lack of research on young people's experience of digital health.	Lupton, D (2021) Young people's use of digital health technologies in the global north: Narrative review. *Journal of Medical Internet Research*, 23(1): p.e18286.

2 Numeric/footnote system

The main numeric referencing styles are British Standard, Vancouver and Chicago. In these systems you should use a sequence of numbers in the body of your assignment. In your list of references (which you might need to put at the end of each page), you should list the sources using your number sequence. You will often also be required to list all sources alphabetically by author family name.

Example using British Standard (numeric) system

In the body of your writing	In your list of references
There is a lack of research on young people's experience of digital health [1].	1. Lupton, D Young people's use of digital health technologies in the global north: Narrative review. *Journal of Medical Internet Research,* 2021, 23:1, e18286.

Your course may have its own variation of a particular referencing style, so always check this with your tutor or course handbook. Your library should be able to recommend software you can use on your draft paper to check that your in-text references are in the correct style.

The difference between a reference list and a bibliography

The list of sources with their publication details at the end of your assignment is referred to as a 'List of References' or 'Bibliography'. Strictly speaking, there is a difference between these two; a reference list should contain only those sources you have used in your writing, whereas a bibliography may also include 'background' sources you have read to help inform your ideas.

Using referencing to emphasise different aspects of your source

1 Emphasising the information

If you want to emphasise the idea/information in your source rather than the author, give the in-text reference at the end of the sentence in brackets:

An improved version of the grey wolf optimizer algorithm uses a dimension inspired by the wolf's learning-based hunting search strategy (Nadimi-Shahraki et al. 2021).

You can also use this method when you want to group key sources:

One relatively new and powerful optimisation problem algorithm is that based on an artificial bee colony (Karaboga 2005, Karaboga and Basturk 2007, 2008, Tsai et al. 2009, Zhu and Kwong 2010).

2 Emphasising both the information and the author

To emphasise the information and the author equally, refer to the fact that research has been done and, as above, give the reference at the end of the sentence using brackets.

> A recent paper proposes an improved version of the grey wolf optimizer algorithm that uses a dimension inspired by the wolf's learning-based hunting search strategy (Nadimi-Shahraki et al. 2021).

You can also use the passive voice:

> An improved version of the grey wolf optimizer algorithm **has been proposed** that uses a dimension inspired by the wolf's learning-based hunting search strategy (Nadimi-Shahraki et al. 2021).

3 Emphasising the author

If you want to emphasise the author of the source, use them as the subject of your sentence, and only put the year of publication/reference number in brackets.

> Nadimi-Shahraki et al. (2021) have proposed an improved version of the grey wolf optimizer algorithm that incorporates a dimension inspired by the wolf's learning-based hunting search strategy.

Check your in-text references

According to (Smith, Rogowski and Lake 2020) insufficient time for care can increase neonatal nurses' intention to quit. ✗	The authors' names should be part of the sentence and so not put in brackets.
According to Padash 2000 there is no strong evidence of long-term damage to health. ✗	*2000* should be in brackets.
Antonio Pea (2021) and others have looked at the role of ncRNAs in cell regulatory systems. ✗	Don't use the author's first name, just their family name.
A strong economy relies on moderate taxation methods (Sloman, Guest and Garratt 2018, *Economics* 10th edn). ✗	In a first mention you might want to include the source title, but never give edition details.
Smoking and related illnesses cause over 700,000 deaths annually in mainland China. ✗	This sentence needs a reference.

Below is a nine-point summary of what to remember in order to avoid accidentally plagiarising in your assignment.

1 No in-text reference = all you

If a sentence does not have a reference, the reader will assume that everything in it is yours – the ideas, information, words, sentence pattern and style. Therefore, if you paraphrase or summarise a source but don't give it a reference, you are plagiarising.

2 It's all or nothing when paraphrasing and summarising

When you paraphrase or summarise source material, you must either change just about everything (except perhaps key terms) or change nothing and use the source as a quotation. Adopting a 'half and half' approach (half your words and half source words) is not acceptable in academic work (see also Chapter 7).

3 Putting a source into your own words is good but make sure you reference it

The information in a paraphrase or source summary comes from the source author not you, so you must always give it a reference.

4 One reference might not be enough

Putting one reference at the end of a paragraph that is a mix of source material and your own points is not enough; you must make clear to your reader where each and every switch is between you and your sources. This means that many of your sentences will need a reference or a 'reference reminder phrase'.

Example: first/main reference

Dickinson (2009) argues that the language translation industry, for example translation brochures and websites, is the key to helping Britain recover from recession. He also goes on to stress the importance of hiring professional translators.

Reference reminder phrase

5 A reference but no quotation marks = paraphrase or summary

Phrases or sentences that have a reference but no quotation marks (or indentation in the case of a long quotation) are assumed by the reader to be your own re-expression of the source, i.e. a paraphrase or source summary. Therefore, if you give a quotation but don't use quotation marks it constitutes plagiarism, because you are giving your reader the impression that you are using your own words and style when in fact they belong to the source author.

6 Reference online material in your assignment

Material from any type of website needs to be referenced in the body of your assignment in the same way as books and other printed sources.

7 Don't give the impression that you have read something when you haven't

If you read a text by author A in which they mention an idea by author B and you want to use author B's idea, you must make clear that you found it in author A's work. To do this you need to use the phrase *cited in*.

In the example below the student makes clear that he has not read Berringer's text but has found their idea in Shaw's article.

> Shaw quotes Berringer to illustrate the point that 'companies will not survive if they do not adapt' (Berringer 2019, cited in Shaw 2021 p. 76).

8 A list of references at the end is not enough

Giving a list of references at the end of your assignment but not referencing in the body of your assignment constitutes plagiarism. This is because any sentence without a reference is assumed to be your own (see point 1 above). You must therefore reference **both** in the body of your assignment each time you use a source and then again in your list of references.

9 Too much use of sources is poor scholarship

Even if you have referenced everything correctly, you can't really claim that you have written an assignment if 80% of it consists of quotation, paraphrase or summary of other people's work.

Summary

- Correct and effective use of source material starts with understanding your source texts well and making notes that record the difference between source words and ideas and your own.

- If you don't understand what a source says, don't use it in your assignment.

- Be clear about why you want to use a source.

- Use a source to support a point you make, not as a substitute for making one.

- Use your own words as often as possible and save quotations for special occasions.

- Avoid accidental plagiarism by remembering the nine referencing rules.

- You will only get credit for your ideas if your tutor can distinguish them from those of your sources, so use referencing and reference reminder phrases to make these distinctions clear.

- Using source material and referencing it correctly is sometimes referred to as 'good scholarship' and having 'academic integrity'. It is the way you show your readers that you are an independent and critical thinker, that you respect other scholars, and that you understand what it means to be part of an academic community.

Notes

For more advice on referencing see *Referencing and Understanding Plagiarism* in this series.
For more advice on using sources and referencing, see *How to Use your Reading in your Essays*
and *Referencing and understanding Plagiarism* in this series.

Here are some phrases from the 'distinction' category of assignment marking criteria:

- *Well argued and clearly focused.*
- *Arguments thoroughly developed.*
- *Extremely well constructed and logically presented argument throughout.*

What your tutors mean by 'an argument'

An academic argument is the whole sequence of stating what you are going to argue or show, using logical reasoning and evidence to do so, and finally giving persuasive conclusions. Not all assignments will have the word 'argue' in the title, but most do require an argument in the broadest sense of the word.

For example, none of the assignment titles below use the word 'argue' but all of them require you to do so:

▶ Civil engineering report: 'Provide an asset strategy for schools in your area.'
▶ Chemistry lab report: 'The effects of pH on enzyme activity.'
▶ Law essay: 'Assess the influence of the Human Rights Act 1998 in the UK.'

As an example of a written argument, below are selected sentences from an academic journal article in the field of computer science.

'A study of the demand for information technology professionals in selected internet job portals.'

As businesses compete in the agile global environment, well-trained information technology (IT) professionals are increasingly important … ↓	**What the authors are doing:** Describing the context for their argument.
Studies found that educators are being blamed for teaching obsolete IT skills because the expertise acquired by graduates is not matching with the needs of companies … ↓	Summarising relevant research.

The primary purpose of this study is to examine the IT job market. Specifically, this study examined the types of expertise needed by new employees …	Stating their overall aims.
↓	
Two internet job databases, Monster.com and HotJobs.com, were selected as the data gathering sources for this study …	Describing their methodology.
↓	
The two hypotheses used were stated as follows: (1): The jobs were equally distributed across all [IT skills] categories. (2): The secondary variable (communication or experience) examined was indicated as a critical expertise …	Stating their specific claims.
↓	
The following table shows the classified outcomes from the 300 jobs. The category that has the largest number of job skills was programming languages …	Describing and analysing their findings.
↓	

Based on the data the first hypothesis was rejected … The second hypothesis produced mixed results …	Evaluating their findings.
↓	
One of the most interesting outcomes obtained in this study is the low to almost non-existence in market demand for traditional programming languages, mainframe and IBM related expertise …	Drawing conclusions from their findings.
↓	
First, individuals who have graduated must participate in continuous education to maintain their marketability …	Discussing the implications of their conclusions.

Adapted extracts from: Koong KS, Liu LC and Liu X (2020) A study of the demand for information technology professionals in selected internet job portals. *Journal of Information Systems Education*, 13(1): 21–8.

What your tutors mean by 'originality'

Here are some more phrases from the 'distinction' or 'excellent' sections of some assignment marking criteria:

- *Selection of sources, ideas, methods brought to bear with original insight.*
- *Able to synthesise and employ ideas in an original way.*
- *Makes an original contribution to the issue.*

At undergraduate level, you can be original in the way you approach your assignment title, the sources you use, how you use them and the conclusions you reach. As an example, below are the conclusions from three student essays all addressing the same essay title: 'Why do consumers buy organic and health foods?'

1 *As this essay has shown, many consumers buy organic produce due mainly to two factors that are of roughly equal importance; the perceived health benefits and the idea that organic farming is less damaging to the environment.*

2 *The conclusion of many of the current studies in this area is that the majority of people buy organic food because they think it is healthier and safer, with more nutrients and fewer pesticides. However, I have suggested above that other factors have been minimised and that if a higher level overview analysis of these*

small-scale studies were conducted, it would probably provide a more nuanced perspective.

3 *This paper has discussed the fact that much of the food consumption literature focuses on health and safety as the main factors that contribute to sales of organic produce. By looking further afield, however, and taking into account studies from other areas of consumer behaviour, this essay has also shown that the 'trendiness', 'fad' and 'peer pressure' factors are also crucial, and that their influence has often been overlooked.*

The three conclusions above all differ from each. Moreover, conclusions two and three show some originality because the students have thought about the question a bit more deeply. Conclusion three is perhaps the most original. Here the student brings together ideas and data from three different areas – studies on consumers and organic food, consumer behaviour in general, and on the effects of trends and peer pressure. Bringing things together like this is called 'synthesis', and by connecting these different areas the student has been able to reach an original insight.

As a final-year undergraduate year or postgraduate student, your assignments are opportunities for you to do even more in-depth thinking, allowing you to make a

contribution (however small) to the ideas and knowledge in your field. You can do this in one or more of the following ways:

1 Adding to current knowledge by confirming, refining or extending what researchers have done up to now.

Example:

Conclusion from an MSc Civil Engineering dissertation

The research in this paper has shown that even though project risks can be presented and mitigated via risk registers, the typical risk register document has limitations, and we have proposed two amendments or additions to the risk register template, which our data suggests can increase effective risk cover levels.

2 Applying a research methodology to a new area or in a new way.

Example:

Conclusion from an MSc Electronics dissertation

Our paper has investigated a novel use of small adjustable magnets, namely to enhance the output of power electronic converters within the context of the increasing use in the industry of wide-bandgap semiconductors.

3 **Comparing sources that have not been brought together before.**

Example:

Conclusion from an MSc dissertation in computing

The proposed 'Youread' app combines what we term a 'personal deep learning algorithm' (PDLA) with authorized access to the client mobile or personal device photo gallery, and 'learns' about the client's recent interests and experiences. Youread uses this data to conduct a targeted internet search, producing a personalized list of podcast and/or book recommendations.

As Bryan Greetham, an expert on creative thinking in academic study, puts it:
analysing a key concept is not just essential in finding an original solution to a problem, but, equally important, in finding an original problem. Your research doesn't have to be ground-breaking. It may just be that in your analysis ... you see things that others have failed to see or failed to pay enough attention to (Greetham 2016 pp. 113–14).

The voice your tutor most wants to see in your assignment is yours; they want to know what you consider to be most important and why. The last chapter looked at how to develop an original argument, but you also need to make sure that it stands out. Ways of doing this include:

▶ clear and correct referencing that shows which ideas are yours and which aren't (see Chapters 6–10).

▶ a sound, clear and well-structured argument and a precise writing style (see Chapters 16–19).

The next few chapters will take you through language points that are also crucial for making your voice clear to your reader.

Showing how your sources support your point

A crucial part of making your voice clear to your reader is to show them why you have used your source material. Below is an essay extract that is weak because the student doesn't say how their sources relate to their own point.

Baber (2006) states that corporations using portable devices should ensure their administrators have had training in computer and network security. Both Bulmer (2007) and Patel (2009) suggest that ongoing staff training programmes are important.

An example of clear student voice

Below is an improved version of the essay extract, in which the student shows the reader why they have used their sources and what their own position is. Chapters 13–15 will show you how to use the aspects of language highlighted.

> Baber (2006) demonstrates that corporations using portable devices should ensure that their system administrators have had training in computer and network security.

The student uses a 'positive' reporting verb to indicate that they agree with Baber.

> I would argue that although this is crucial, it is probably just as important to have a programme of *ongoing* staff training as part of an organised educational approach.

The student shows how they agree with Baber but that their own argument goes further.

Shows a high degree of certainty (but not absolute).

> The usefulness of such programmes has been shown in two key studies conducted by Bulmer (2007) and Patel (2009).

The student shows why they are using Bulmer and Patel.

13   Using verbs to show your own position

Using reporting verbs to show what you think about a source

Chapter 8 looked at using verbs to show that you understand what a source author is doing in their text. The other important function of reporting verbs is to show what *you* think and what *your* position is in relation to the source author's ideas.

Read the extract below from an article by Deborah Lupton (2021):

> The reviewed research has found that many young people in the Global North are active users of digital health technologies. However, it is notable that they still rely on older technologies, such as websites and search engines, to find information.
>
> Lupton D (2021) Young people's use of digital health technologies in the global north: Narrative review. *Journal of Medical Internet Research*, 23(1): p.e18286.

If you shared Lupton's view and wanted to indicate this in your assignment, you might use a 'positive' verb such as *show* to introduce what she says and then go on to agree with her:

> Lupton (2021) *shows* that young people still tend to use traditional search engines and website platforms for health-related content. This idea is supported by other studies suggesting that …

However, if you wanted to argue against Lupton, you would need to use a more 'open' verb such as *assert*:

> Lupton (2021) *asserts* that young people still tend to use traditional search engines and website platforms for health-related content. However, there is some contradictory data to suggest that …

Positive verbs		Open verbs	
confirm	illustrate	argue	discuss
convey	note	assert	examine
demonstrate	observe	assume	give
describe	point out	claim	maintain
establish	show	conclude	state
find		contend	suggest

So, positive verbs show that you agree with the author, whereas 'open' verbs leave the door open for you to then agree or disagree.

Other language for showing your position towards a source

Indicating a positive position	Indicating a negative position

Zhu's research …
    benefits from
    considers all aspects
    correctly identifies
    examines in great detail
 	
Zhu's research is …
    conclusive
    important
    interesting
    reliable
    sound
    valid
	Zhu's research …
	    fails to consider
	    neglects the fact that
	    overlooks
	    suffers from
	    wrongly assumes
	
	Zhu's research is …
	    flawed
	    inconclusive
	    limited
	    questionable
	    unreliable
	    unsatisfactory

Using 'I'

Using 'I' is increasingly acceptable in some academic disciplines as a way of showing your tutor your voice and position, particularly in the introductory and concluding sections of an assignment and in reflective writing tasks. However, be careful what you use *after* 'I' – don't fall into the trap of using it to start giving personal opinions or to write in a chatty style. In academic study, you usually need to earn the right to use 'I' by first analysing and evaluating your sources and only then using it to give your informed and supported viewpoint. Check with your tutor if you are not sure what is acceptable on your course.

When to use 'I'	Examples ✔
When you want to state what you will do or have done.	*I will attempt to show that …* *I will examine/argue/suggest/propose …* *I have demonstrated that …*
To evaluate a source or to state/clarify your position.	*I would suggest that these findings are important and would add that …*
When your assignment requires reflective writing.	*I think that the experiment would have been better if …*

When not to use 'I'	Examples ✗
To give a personal opinion that is not supported (or is even contradicted) by the evidence – this is not acceptable.	*I feel discouraged by the current state of the environment.* *I think that we should all work until at least 65.* *I don't like animal testing because …* *The study indicates that homeopathy is not effective, but I still feel that it works.* *I believe in the power of the mind.*
To describe methodology, stages and processes where it is not important who did what. Instead, use the passive form: *The equipment was washed in saline solution*.	*I washed the equipment in saline solution.*
To give information or to state a fact. Instead just give the fact: *Dickens was born in 1812.*	*I read that Dickens was born in 1812.*

Using 'we'

Students sometimes overuse 'we' because they are trying not to use 'I' and because they think they should use the formal use of 'we' meaning 'I'. However, tutors increasingly prefer students to use 'we' only when referring to a genuine plural.

When to use 'we'	Example ✔
To indicate collaborative and/or teamwork	*We each interviewed 10 students.*
In a group presentation	*We will begin by …* *We would like to point out that …*

When not to use 'we'	Examples ✗
To refer to both you and the reader This can be ambiguous (do you mean you, you and the reader, or a team?) and also sounds as if you are telling the reader what to think. Instead use phrases such as: *It should be noted that … /Table 5 shows that …* *I suggest that the data shows a link …*	*We should note that …* *We need to consider the data from …* *We can see from Table 5 that …* *From this we can infer a link between …*

When not to use 'we'	Examples ✗
To refer to society/everyone	
'We' used in this way is often an overgeneralisation. (See also Chapter 5.) It's better to: simply state the fact (*smoking is addictive*) or use the passive form and avoid the verb 'know' (*the addictive nature of smoking is well established*).	*As we (all) know, smoking is addictive.* *We all want to live in a fairer society.*
Using 'we' to talk about actions is usually too informal and personal for academic writing. Instead use nouns (*Deforestation causes ...)* (see Chapter 18).	*When we cut down forests we cause ...*

Be wary of expressing absolute certainty, for example:

The data proves the existence of automatic ageism.
Removing speed cameras will result in an increase in the number of road deaths.
Children are definitely more aware politically than in previous generations.

Even though you think there is overwhelming evidence to support a statement, someone else may think differently, and even the most eminent experts on a subject accept that they might be wrong. Textbooks tend to simplify perspectives on knowledge, but if you look at an academic journal article in your subject area, you will see that authors use words and phrases such as *probably* and *this might suggest* to add a degree of caution to their claim. In academic study, all knowledge is contestable and something that can only be proven false, not true.

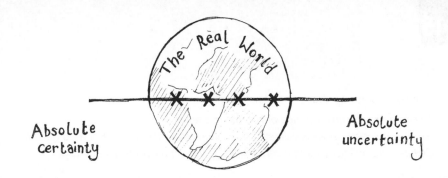

Absolute certainty

Absolute uncertainty

You can show this contestable nature of knowledge by using 'cautious' language such as *I suggest, this might indicate, this indicates a tendency, it is probably*. An additional benefit of using cautious language is that it helps persuade your reader rather than sounding as if you are telling them what to think.

Below are phrases ordered according to their certainty level. Use them in your own writing to indicate how certain you are about something and to acknowledge the contestable nature of knowledge.

Verb phrases

certainty

The data shows
The findings indicate/suggest/tend to show
The data seems/appears to
There appears/seems to be
This might/may/could indicate
caution   This would seem to/appear to

Adverb/verb phrases

certainty   This strongly/certainly/definitely suggests
This almost certainly/definitely suggests/shows/indicates
I would strongly suggest
caution   This perhaps suggests

Adjective/noun phrases

certainty

This proves with absolute certainty

It is almost certain/highly probable

There is a good/strong/definite possibility

It is probable/likely

There is a tendency for

It is possible

caution

There is a slight/small possibility

NB: Some tutors don't like the use of verbs such as *suggests* for inanimate objects (e.g. *The data suggests ...*).

Summary

- Get really involved in your assignment at a deep, critical level.
- Produce an original piece of work by making your own connections between different source perspectives to create new insights and concepts.
- The loudest argument and written voice should be your own, so make it stand out.
- Be precise in your use of reporting verbs both to show your understanding of the sources and your own position in relation to them.
- Don't write like a textbook – your tutor wants to see that you appreciate the contestable nature of knowledge, so use language to express appropriate degrees of caution or certainty.

Notes

For more on smart thinking, analysis and creating new concepts, see *Smart Thinking* in the References.

WRITE FOR YOUR READER

You can't be there when your tutor reads your assignment, and they might not go back to reread a section that they didn't understand the first time. So, a successful piece of writing has good content but also needs a clear structure and a precise written style. In this book we have already looked at ways of developing content through critical thinking, argument development and effective use of source material. In the next few chapters we will look at structure and style.

16 Creating a clear assignment structure

You need to structure your writing clearly in order for your ideas to shine. Most types of assignment should have the following basic components:

▶ an introduction
▶ some review of relevant key literature
▶ the main body (including methodology and results sections if relevant)
▶ a discussion and/or concluding section.

The detailed structure of your assignment within these broad categories should be driven by the assignment type, how you interpret the issue or question (see Chapter 3) and your argument. Chapter 11 looked at argument development, using key sentences from a computer science report as an example. If you look at this example on p. 70 again, you will see that the way the authors develop their argument goes hand in hand with its structure.

Below is another example of assignment structure, this time using the first sentence from each paragraph of a second-year undergraduate discursive essay. The annotations on the right describe the structural aspects of this essay.

Outline what business ethics is and discuss whether it is important. (2,500 words)

Over the past couple of decades, the issue of the ethical stance of businesses appears to have become more explicitly an area of public debate and consumer awareness. Two illustrations of this are …	**INTRODUCTION – say what you are going to do** Introduce the issue or question in an interesting way that shows and/or states that it is important.
There are numerous, overlapping definitions of business ethics. Shaw and Barry (2007) see it as …	Define key terms if necessary and state the scope of your paper, perhaps saying what you will and will *not* cover and why.
Combining all the perspectives outlined above, my own definition of business ethics as …	**Review of key literature** Summarise, group and connect relevant key literature to give the reader a picture of current research on the issue, stating how your work fits into this context.
Views differ as to whether ethics have a valid place in business, ranging from …	
In this essay then, I argue against those who see business ethics as irrelevant and suggest that ethics are essential to businesses for four interrelated reasons.	**Outline what you are going to discuss and the order in which you will do so.**

Creating a clear assignment structure

The first of my four points, then, is that ...	**BODY – do what you said you would do in your introduction**
A consideration of ... is the second rationale I give for the need for ...	Start to explore the issue and develop your argument by making logical steps supported by sources.
The third reason ...	
We now come to the final aspect of ethical business practices that appears to be ...	
As I have shown, the four reasons I give for the relevance of business ethics all seem to stem from the fact that ...	Continue to explore and develop the issue.
The key underlying factor that seems to connect all of these various aspects is, I argue ...	Clarify what you feel is at the heart of the position you have arrived at.
This paper has demonstrated that ...	**CONCLUSION – say what you have done**
I would in fact go further and suggest that unless businesses ...	Bring things together and clarify the position you have arrived at and why.
Questions remain as to what ...	If possible, push further and identify extra dimensions and distinctions within the issue.
	Suggest interesting ideas and/or questions for future research on the issue.

Planning and checking the structure of your assignment

A useful way of doing this is to write out or cut and paste what you think will be the first sentence in each paragraph to create a 'topic sentence skeleton'. Use this skeleton to check that the theme of each paragraph is relevant to the assignment as a whole and that the paragraphs are in a logical order.

As an example, below are the first sentences from paragraphs 1–5 of the business ethics essay.

Outline what business ethics is and discuss whether it is important. (2,500 words)

Topic sentence of the paragraph	General topic of the paragraph	Specific topic of the paragraph
Over the past couple of decades, the issue of the ethical stance of businesses appears to have become more explicitly an area of public debate and consumer awareness.	Business ethics	Introduction to the topic of business ethics (BE).

There are numerous, overlapping definitions of business ethics. Shaw and Barry (2007) see it as ...	Business ethics	Definitions of BE.
Combining all the perspectives outlined above, my own definition of business ethics is ...	Business ethics	Student's own definition of BE.
Views differ as to whether ethics have a valid place in business, ranging from ...	Business ethics	Review of different views on importance of BE in the literature.
In this essay then, I argue against those who see business ethics as irrelevant and suggest that ethics are essential to businesses for four interrelated reasons.	Business ethics	Student's thesis statement.

This idea is adapted from one created by the Excelsior Online Writing Lab, https://owl.excelsior.edu/writing-process/paragraphing/paragraphing-topic-sentences/.

Use some signposting language

Language 'signposts' help guide your reader through your work, but remember that the most important way to create a clear structure is through the logical order of your content. Indeed, you can write well using only a few signpost phrases; for example, in the topic sentence skeleton above, only paragraph five begins with a signpost phrase (*In this essay then …*).

So, **don't** use signposting phrases in an attempt to cover up a lack of good content, but **do use them** to make clear to your reader how your points connect, contrast and develop.

Signpost phrases

Saying what you are going to do/order points
In this essay I will … / This essay will …
first, second, third, next, then
Adding another similar point
In addition/An additional x is
Another x is
Also/As well as x there is
Moreover/Furthermore/Similarly

What is more
Moving on to a contrasting point
In contrast/By contrast/Conversely
Moving on to a different point
As for/Regarding/With regard to
Moving on to/With respect to
Restating/rephrasing
In other words/That is to say
Put another way/To put it more simply

Introducing alternative views

Alternatively/A different interpretation is

A different viewpoint could be

An opposing view is/Others argue that

It could also be argued that

Concluding

To conclude/In conclusion/To summarise

Reasoning:

Cause/result

Because/Since/Therefore/Thus

So as/This means that

This results in/As a result

Consequently/The effect of this is

This suggests that

Contrasting

But/However/Yet

On the contrary/In contrast

Concession

Nevertheless/Despite x it is still

Although/However

Similarity

Similarly/Likewise/In the same way

Condition

Unless/Provided that/If/As long as

2nd Main Issue

17 Structuring paragraphs

The last chapter looked at creating a clear assignment structure, but this can only be achieved if each paragraph within this overall structure is also well constructed.

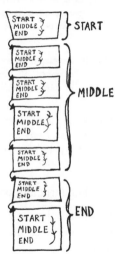

A paragraph is a section of text that deals with one main point or idea, and it is marked in a text by an indented first line or by a line space. The precise content and function of a paragraph will vary according to the type of assignment and its place within it, but they should all have some kind of beginning, middle and end.

Each paragraph should provide the reader with a digestible chunk of the text's 'conversation', allowing them to pause at the end of the paragraph and think 'ok, I get that' before moving on to the next section.

The essentials of paragraph structure

Start: a topic sentence that gives the idea or theme of that specific paragraph and (perhaps) also links explicitly to the previous paragraph.

Middle: development of this idea via one or more of evidence, explanation or discussion.

End: a comment on the evidence and/or a restatement or clarification of the paragraph's point and (perhaps) also an explicit link to the next one.

Creating structure within and between paragraphs

Below is an extract from the methodology section of an engineering dissertation report, in which the student describes and discusses the research models they have used. The annotations on the right show how the student has created the structure of the paragraphs and made links between them. Note that even in an assignment that uses subheadings, each section should consist of a well-structured paragraph.

6.3 The Rasch Model *… and so this was felt to be the most relevant* *and useful model to use in for our analysis.*	**End** – the last sentence of this paragraph gives a mini conclusion, summarising and 'wrapping up' the point of the section.
6.4 Item Response Theory *To effectively understand the Rasch Model it is important to also understand the key underlying theory on which it is based, namely Item Response Theory, also known as IRT. This theory comprises a set of mathematical models that describe the relationship between the performances of test subjects of a given ability to each item in the test.*	**Start** – this first sentence in this paragraph gives an explicit link to the previous section ('the Rasch Model') and also provides the topic sentence for this one.
The basis of IRT is that the probability of a correct response to an item is a direct mathematical function of person and item parameters. An example of a person parameter could be intelligence and an example of an item parameter could be its difficulty.	**Middle** – explanation of what the Rasch Model is based on (IRT) and what IRT is.
In general terms, IRT entails a number of different models which are defined by the number of item parameters it contains.	**End** – This last sentence concludes the paragraph by giving a summary definition of IRT.
6.5 How the Rasch Model was used in the experiment *In the current paper the Rasch Model was used to …*	**Start** – The content of this paragraph and section follows on logically from the previous one and so no explicit linking phrase is needed.

You might also like to look back at the essay extract on organic and health foods in Chapter 2, page 7, which also has annotations that comment on paragraph structure.

Paragraph length

The length of a paragraph depends on its function but, as a general rule, it should be at least three sentences long. If you find you have a paragraph of only one or two sentences, you probably need to either develop the idea more, provide an example or evidence, move it into another paragraph, or get rid of it. At the other end of the scale, avoid paragraphs that are more than half a page because long, unbroken sections might be hard for your reader to digest. If you are conveying a complex idea, you will need to break it down into smaller subunits and allocate a paragraph to each one.

This book has already covered many aspects essential for clear and precise writing:

- using evidence and logic to argue rather than giving personal opinion (pp. 21–31)
- being objective and neutral (pp. 21–31)
- being specific (pp. 26–31 and 87–91)
- using source material correctly and effectively (pp. 33–68)
- using appropriate verbs and other phrases to report and evaluate sources (pp. 52–56, 80–82 and p. 89)
- using 'I' and 'we' appropriately (pp. 83–86)
- using cautious language (pp. 87–90)
- using content and signposting phrases to structure your writing (pp. 97–100).

The rest of this chapter will take you through further features of language you can use to develop an appropriate writing style.

The right level of formality

✗ Don't use:
Contractions – *it's, can't, won't.*
Word abbreviations – *dept., gov. e.g., i.e.* You might be able to use *e.g.* and *i.e.* inside brackets, but check this with your tutor.
Vague 'run-on' expressions – *etc., and so on, and so forth,* e.g. *A healthy lifestyle means eating well, exercising and so forth.*
Direct questions, e.g. *So, what are the main causes of global warming?* An occasional question for impact is okay, but they can make your writing look informal.
'You' to address the reader, e.g. *You probably know about the current research,* or to give the reader orders, e.g. *You need to consider the issue carefully.*
Rude or emotional adjectives, e.g. *awful, ridiculous, stupid, pretty, terrible, unfair.*
Vague words such as *stuff* or *thing.*
Informal quantities – *a bit, a lot of, plenty of, huge.*
The verb *get,* or too many two-part verbs, e.g. *cut down, make up, got worse, brought up, set up, look into, put up with, find out.*

> **✓ Do use:**
>
> Full word forms – *it is*, *cannot*, *will not*.
>
> Correct punctuation, as you need this to convey your meaning clearly.
>
> Precise endings for your sentences, e.g. *A healthy lifestyle means eating well, exercising, a good work–life balance and a generally healthy environment.*
>
> Acronyms e.g. *WHO*, but the first time you use one, give the full form followed by the acronym in brackets, e.g. *World Health Organization (WHO)*
>
> Precise descriptions of things, e.g. *theory, idea, action, issue, chemical.*
>
> Precise, formal equivalents for two-part verbs, e.g. *reduce, compensate, worsened, raised, established, investigate, tolerate, discover.*

For more advice on good writing style, see *Brilliant writing tips for students* in this series.

Speech-like phrases and clichés

Don't use these, as they informal and also often vague or meaningless; it's much better to explain exactly what you want to say in your own words.

✗ Don't use:

along the way

anyway

at first

at last

at the end of the day

basically

in a nutshell

in the end

it all comes down to

last but not least

a different ball game

beyond a shadow of a doubt

easier said than done

keep a lid on

leave no stone unturned

see the light at the end of the tunnel

that's another story

the thing is

to name but a few

to put it mildly

Use nouns to emphasise key concepts

Academic writing is quite dense and powerful – it packs a lot of information into a small amount of text. In your writing you will need to emphasise ideas, qualities, facts or actions. Rather than convey these things using subject + verb phrases, e.g. *people don't have jobs*, it will help your reader if you express them as nouns, e.g. *unemployment*. The two versions of the essay extract below show you what I mean:

Version A ✗ – less clear

The doctor will choose which drug to treat the patient with, depending on whether *they have had* previous health problems and *what they do* for a living. If *they are someone who is* resistant to penicillin, *the doctor will also need* to do a skin test so that *they can check* for *reactions that might cause* problems.

Subject + verb phrases – these are distracting, as the reader doesn't need to think about individual doctors or patients. Also, the main concepts are lost in the middle of the sentences.

Version B ✓ – clear and precise

The treatment drug depends on the *patient's medical history* and *current occupation*. *Penicillin-resistant patients* will also need a skin test to check for *potential negative reactions*.

Noun phrases – this way of expressing the main ideas makes them stand out clearly at the beginning of each sentence, and so the extract is more succinct and powerful.

Use verbs in the passive form ...

If you are emphasising specific or individual actions, you will sometimes need to express them as verbs. In academic writing, the passive form is often used in order to emphasise the action rather than the person/people, e.g. The study *has been replicated* several times, with consistent results.

... but also use the active form

Using the passive form too much, however, can make your writing overly complicated and vague, and tutors increasingly like to see a more direct writing style that uses active verb forms or just gives the statement directly, particularly when referring to your own actions and opinions.

Passive verb forms ✗	Active verb forms ✓
It has been argued in this essay that ... It is now required by the government that all ... It needs to be emphasised that this theory is flawed ...	I have argued in this essay that ... The government now requires all ... This theory is flawed ...

The appropriate balance of passive and active verb forms depends on your discipline, your assignment, the assignment section and on tutor preference, so if you are not sure about which form to use, check with your tutor.

Strike the right balance of sentence length

The most important thing is that your sentences are clear and convey your ideas with precision. Avoid sentences that have more than about 35 words or more than two parts (the odd sentence with three parts is okay). Your writing should also flow smoothly and have a sense of connection, so avoid having a series of very short sentences.

⊠ One sentence – too long

Online translation programmes work via what would seem to be the same process as a human translator, which is to read each word, but the machine does not understand the text content, and it also does not consider the register and context, producing incomprehensible translation that is difficult to read.

⊠ Six sentences – too short

Online translation programmes work via what would seem to be the same process as a human translator. This process is to read each word. A machine does not understand the text content. It also does not consider the register and context. Because a machine cannot do these things it produces incomprehensible translation. This translation is difficult to read.

☑ Two sentences – okay

Online translation programmes work via what would seem to be the same process as a human translator, which is to read each word. The difference is that a machine does not understand the text content and does not consider the register and context, producing incomprehensible translation that is difficult to read.

Be succinct

Good academic writing is precise and to the point. Writing in a formal style and discussing complex ideas does *not* mean that you have to use as many 'long words' as possible, and academic articles that do so are probably poorly written.

You will need to use a fairly formal style of vocabulary in order to be precise, but avoid words that are overly complicated.

Examples:
This essay will *commence with* ✗/*start with* ✓
The tower *was fabricated in* ✗/*built in* ✓
We *utilised* ✗/*used* ✓ three different methods.

Also avoid words that merely repeat the previous one.

Examples:

absolutely essential ✗ – essential ✓

conclusive proof ✗ – proof ✓

hard evidence ✗ – evidence ✓

different varieties ✗ – varieties ✓

or, alternatively ✗ – alternatively ✓

past history ✗ – history ✓

revert back to ✗ – revert to ✓

close proximity ✗ – proximity ✓

join together ✗ – join ✓

true facts ✗ – facts ✓

Be authentic

Don't copy someone else's style or use words you don't fully understand; your tutor would rather see you explain your ideas clearly in less formal words than unclearly in someone else's complicated language. If you find you can't write clearly about something, it might be because you are not sure what you want to say, and need to do some more reading and thinking first.

The main reason for using more formal vocabulary is that it is precise and therefore powerful, enabling you to explain even complex ideas accurately. It is, however, all too easy to use the wrong word in a 'nearly but not quite right' way.

Examples:

There is a distinct range of ethnic groups in London. (diverse)

Pollution from the new factories has exaggerated the problem. (exacerbated)

Polio vaccinations in the 1960s had virtually prevented the disease by the 1970s. (eliminated/eradicated)

The data infers that lack of sunlight increases risk of depression. (indicate)

The UK population is generally 60,000,000. (approximately)

Most people need to continue to build their vocabulary knowledge as they progress in their studies and career. Use some of the vocabulary learning strategies below to help develop your ability to use words precisely in your writing:

- Note down words that you think are useful and/or that keep cropping up in your reading. If you are not sure which are the most useful words to learn, look up online guides and dictionaries that give you lists of 'common academic vocabulary' and use online subject dictionaries, glossaries and lists of key terms in your subject to develop your discipline-specific word knowledge.*

- Look up words in a good English-English dictionary, preferably one that gives the word in example sentences. When you look up a word, take note of the information it gives about grammar and style and, importantly, which other words are commonly used with the key word – there are 'collocation dictionaries' that give this information.*

- Learn the different forms of key words (adjective, noun, verb, adverb) and practise using them in your writing.

*See the list of Useful sources.

Summary

- It's your job to make your assignment easy to read; put yourself in your reader's shoes.
- Check that you understand the purpose of the type of assignment as well as the specific task.
- Each paragraph should have its own logical structure.
- Use a 'topic sentence skeleton' to check your content and structure.
- Don't try to hide poor content or confused ideas behind signpost phrases or complicated vocabulary.
- It's better to write clearly using simple language than to express things poorly using more complex words.
- Use words precisely and never use a word you don't fully understand.
- Developing a clear writing style takes time.

For more advice on essay planning and structure, see *Planning your Essay* in this series.

Brilliant assignments are usually the result of a lot of reading, thinking, planning, drafting, redrafting (making larger changes) and proofreading (making smaller, 'surface' amendments). When you start thinking and reading for an assignment, keep an open and questioning mind – you should continue to develop your argument, viewpoints and conclusions as you research and write your first and perhaps second draft. In these drafts then, you will probably be writing more for yourself than for your reader. By the time you reach the stage of producing your third and/or final draft, however, you should have a clear and informed position that you should convey logically, clearly and precisely with your reader in mind.

Below is a checklist to remind you of the different aspects and stages involved in producing an effective piece of writing. In reality, producing your assignment will probably be a 'back and forth' process between these stages, so don't feel that you have to stick rigidly to the sequence outlined here.

First draft

Ignore grammar and minor mistakes. Ask yourself:

▶ What are my draft's overall strengths and weaknesses?
▶ Does my argument make sense?
▶ Have I answered the assignment title/brief?
▶ Are there any content gaps or irrelevancies?
▶ Should anything be in a different order?
▶ Do I need to do any of the following: additional research, more thinking, rewrite any sections, adjust my final position?
▶ Do I need to clarify anything about the assignment with my tutor?

! Top tip
Don't write your introduction until your second draft, when you are more sure about the content and order of your body and conclusion.

Second draft

Check all of the above again and also ask yourself:

▶ Do my introduction and conclusion match up?
▶ Does my conclusion *really* answer the assignment title, the full title and only the title?
▶ Is the content of each paragraph relevant to the assignment title?
▶ Do I indicate clearly at the start of each paragraph what it's about?
▶ Are any paragraphs too long or too short?
▶ Have I given a reference or reminder phrase every time I use a source?
▶ Is *my* argument and voice the dominant one?
▶ Would my reader find my draft clear, logical and easy to read?

Third/final draft

Read your draft aloud and slowly, and check:

▶ Could the structure and flow between paragraphs still be more logical?
▶ Will the meaning of each sentence be clear to my reader?
▶ Could I make any points even more precise and persuasive?

Proofreading and polishing

When you think you have finished making larger changes to your draft, it's time to make smaller amendments and to give your piece a final polish. Checking for small, 'surface' errors and typos, and making small corrections to the format and reference list is called 'proofreading'.

Check for common grammar mistakes

In your final draft, check for grammar errors that might make your meaning less clear. Don't rely on computer software and apps to do this for you, as they can only identify a limited range of errors and are not always right – you really do need to proofread your work using your own eyes and brain.

Below is a list of the most common errors to check for, with the grammatical terminology given in brackets for your reference.

1 Wrong form of the word (adjective, noun, verb, adverb)

Countries are making changes to suit tourisms / tourists.

There is still a potentially / potential market.

2 Sentences that are missing a main verb or clause (fragment sentences)

~~Although there are several advantages.~~ ✓

Although there are several advantages, there is also one major drawback.

~~The experiment, which was conducted by a team in London.~~ ✓

The experiment, which was conducted by a team in London, will be published next week.

3 Joined sentences that should be separated (run-on/fused sentences)

These decisions can have significant implications, ✗ most managers do not receive adequate training. *To correct, replace the comma with either a semi-colon or a full stop.*

The web is a constantly developing technology, ✗ this can cause data security problems. *To correct, replace the comma with either a semi-colon or a full stop.*

4 Using the wrong logical connector

Avery (2009) and Hallam (2016) have found that consumers are concerned with pesticide use; moreover, ✗ / however, ✓ a more recent study by Wong (2021) reveals a different picture.

5 Incorrectly using commas with that

The only time you should use a comma before or after *that* is in the phrase *that is*.

It has been shown in this essay that, ✗ this is not the case.

It is illogical, ✗ that people think pollution is not important.

My meeting is on the fourth, that ✓ is, Tuesday.

6 Incorrect use of commas with which/who (relative clauses)

If the *which/who* part of your sentence is **essential information**, so do not use commas:

Key authors who disagree with Ashol are Mahones (2017) and Lui (2021).

If the *which/who* part of your sentence is **additional information**, do use commas to separate this information from the main clause:

Ogbe and Affika (2021), who disagree with Selle (2007), propose a refocusing of research in poultry nutrition and health.

Tourist crisis management, which has become increasingly urgent, comprises the plans and measures needed within the industry to react swiftly to disaster events.

7 Incorrect switches in verb tense

You can use more than one verb tense in a sentence …

Avery (2006) and Hallam (2003) have found that consumers are concerned about pesticide use, but a more recent study by Wong (2021) reveals a different picture.

but be careful not to mix tenses that should have the same time frame:

The solution was put into the test tube and has been heated/was heated to …

8 Incorrect mix of singular and plural for the subject and verb (subject–verb agreement)

Smith et al. (2000) ~~reports~~ / report ✓ that this level of violence is harmful.

Recent research also ~~show~~ / shows ✓ that the drugs are effective.

9 Incorrect use of *the* (definite article)

There are some groups among ~~the society~~ / among society ✓ that object to this research.

The study shows that ~~immune system~~ / that the immune system ✓ is extremely complex.

10 Wrong choice of *to + verb* or *verb + ing* after the key word (infinitive or gerund)

The model is ~~capable to make~~ / capable of making ✓ accurate predictions.

The failure of cells from ~~removing~~ / to remove ✓ sugars causes diabetes.

11 Wrong word before or after the key word (preposition, collocation)

I will ~~discuss about violence~~ / discuss violence ✓ in computer games.

They are both ~~at~~ / in ✓ a constant state of balance.

12 Incorrect sentence structure for direct questions

The issue ~~is if~~ / whether ✓ this will lead to an increase in violence.

Research was conducted ✓ to see ~~what was the cause of the disease~~ / what the cause of the disease was. ✓ / to find the cause of the disease.

13 Incorrectly using commonly confused words

There are two main types of law, such ~~as~~ / namely ✓ criminal and civil.

14 Incorrect use of apostrophes

The apostrophe is never used to indicate a plural, and in formal writing you shouldn't really use short forms (e.g. *do not > don't, it is > it's*), so only use apostrophes to show possession:

The scientific community *of this country* > *this country's* ✓ scientific community

The article *of Dr Ashi* > *Dr Ashi's* ✓ article

If a proper noun ends with an *s*, you can follow the normal rule and write *s's* or drop the second *s*:

The theory of *Dr Jones* > *Dr Jones's* ✓ theory or *Dr Jones'* ✓ theory

Also note that personal pronouns (*his/hers/its/ours/yours/theirs*) do **not** use an apostrophe:

The title is 'Expression' > Its ✓ title is 'Expression'

The controversy over global warming stems from the uncertainty of ~~it's~~ / its ✓ main cause

15 Incorrect use of capital letters

A key concept in the management of ~~Engineering~~ / engineering ✓ projects is risk assessment.

Practise your redrafting and proofreading skills

Below is a paragraph from the second draft of a student essay that needs some redrafting and proofreading. Suggested amendments are given on the right, but you might like to cover them up and have a go at checking the paragraph yourself.

Draft paragraph

The 2007 financial crisis was a product of worldwide globalisation. It can be submitted that a financial crisis results in an increase in the need for litigation, an increase in litigation means financial gain for the law firms. During which the world experienced a boom and bust cycle that no doubt will continue to repeat itself.

Comments

Worldwide is redundant - globalisation is by definition worldwide. Also, the topic sentence has no relevance to the main point of the paragraph, so delete.

An overly formal and inappropriate phrase for an essay (comes from a phrase used in court).

This is a run-on sentence that needs more than a comma.

Sentence is irrelevant, is a fragment, and uses an empty persuader (no doubt).

A review compiled by Anne Lee Gibson, a top American lawyer who specializes in competition law showed that the top 100 Am Law firms total revenue increased by the greatest percent in each of the three years preceding the appearance of the three recessions since 1984.[6] Recession results of debt, however debt can be valuable when a company goes bankrupt as many have in recent recession, lots of trading debts occurs this can result in major profit as it is the lawyers who arrange the trading.

Irrelevant information.

firms should be firms'.

What does 'increased by the greatest percent' mean? percent should be percentage.

Run-on sentences – should be split into two or three separate sentences.

Wrong preposition: in, not of.

Wrong subject-verb agreement. Debts is plural so the verb form should be occur (no s).

You can't just say major profit – should be a significant profit or perhaps large profits.

Give your work a final polish

Top tips

- Try to plan enough time so that you can put your final draft away for a day or two before giving it a final check.
- To help put yourself into your reader's shoes and to see what you have written rather than what you *think* you have written, try one or more of:

    putting your text into a large font (14+) with double spacing and using this version for a final read-through

    reading your work slowly and out loud

    getting someone else to read out your work to you

    recording yourself reading out loud and then playing it back.

And finally, check that you have …

- given a reference or reference reminder phrase each time you have used a source in your writing, and that you have listed them all in your list of references.
- followed the instructions for the assignment format, cover sheet and appendices.

Summary

▶ There is no 'right' or 'best' method for producing a good piece of writing – you can use either a back and forth process or a more linear one.

▶ When writing your first and second draft, concentrate on content, clarity of meaning and persuasiveness rather than minor grammatical errors.

▶ Check and polish your assignment at least three times – it's your job as the author to make your work easy to read.

▶ If your assignment presentation is sloppy, your tutor might feel that you don't care about your work or about the fact that they have to read it, and they might therefore deduct marks, so make sure your formatting and presentation are good.

▶ Good written communication is one of the top five employability skills.

End comments

Your assignments are not separate from your subject but are opportunities to engage with it and think about it more deeply. As you progress through your course, reflect on the ways in which different assignment topics connect to each other, both within and between modules and levels of study. Take action on your tutor feedback so that you can continue to develop as a communicator in your field.

Most importantly, care about what you write and develop a sense of ownership – you are the writer and author of your work and it's your name on the cover sheet. Your individual interpretation of the issue, your choice and evaluation of sources, and the connections and conclusions you come to are what will make your work unique.

Doing these things will help you develop an awareness of where the scholars in your subject position themselves – of where and how brightly their stars shine in your discipline's galaxy. Think of yourself also as a scholar and author in your academic community, and of the fact that your own written pieces identify the position of your own star.

WRITING FOR UNIVERSITY

References

Copus J (2009) *Brilliant Writing tips for Students*. Basingstoke: Palgrave Macmillan.

Excelsior Online Writing Lab (n.d.) Paragraphing, available at: https://owl.excelsior.edu/writing-process/paragraphing/paragraphing-topic-sentences.

Godfrey J (2014) *Reading and Making Notes* (2nd edn). Basingstoke: Palgrave Macmillan.

Godfrey J (2018) *How to Use your Reading in your Essays* (3rd edn). London: Palgrave.

Godwin J (2019) *Planning your Essay* (3rd edn). London: Red Globe Press.

Greetham B (2016) *Smart Thinking: How to Think Conceptually, Design Solutions and Make Decisions*. London: Red Globe Press.

Williams K (2022) *Getting Critical* (3rd edn). London: Bloomsbury.

Williams K and Davis M (2017) *Referencing and Understanding Plagiarism* (2nd edn). London: Palgrave.

Useful sources

Coonan E (2020) *Where's Your Evidence?* London: Red Globe Press.

Godfrey J (2020) *The Student Phrase Book: Vocabulary for Writing at University* (2nd edn). London: Red Globe Press.

Longman Collocations Dictionary and Thesaurus (2013). Pearson Education.

Pears R and Shields G (2019) *Cite them Right: The essential referencing guide* (11th edn). London: Red Globe Press.

University of Manchester (2021) *Academic Phrasebank*. Available at www.phrasebank. manchester.ac.uk/index.htm.

Index